PRO FOOTBALL
PLAYBOOK

Copyright © 2012

All rights reserved.

ISBN: 0984942750

ISBN 13: 9780984942756

This edition published by Bookworm Sports.

For more information, visit www.bookwormsports.com.

PRO FOOTBALL PLAYBOOK

For Predicting Scores and Placing Winning Wagers

By Wall Street Investment Manager
WILLIAM O. HALL, III

Table of Contents

Chapter One: Begin With the Basics   1

                         Proper Preparation   1
                         The Fundamentals — a Review   2
                         Value Ratings   2
                         Score Sheets   6
                         Matchup Analysis   9

Chapter Two: Preseason Preparation   17

                         The Prior Year's Value Ratings Are the Starting Point   17
                         Prior Year Value Rating Adjustments   17
                         The NFL's Law of Gravity   18
                         Don't Despair, It Will Get Better   20
                         Takeaways and Turnarounds   21
                         Score Sheets Show the Lucky, Unlucky and Overrated, and Teams on the Rise   25
                         The Lucky of 2011–12   25
                         The Unlucky of 2011–12   31
                         The Overrated of 2011–12   34
                         2011–12's Team on the Rise   36
                         Run All the Numbers From the Prior Season   39

Chapter Three: Read the Board   41

                         Why Lines Move: Not All Point Spreads Are Equal   43
                         Off-Standard Point Spreads   44
                         Betting on Totals: A Simple Path to Success   45
                         Money Lines: It's Not As Hard as You Think   46
                         Proposition Bets   49
                         Sports Books: The Internet vs. Las Vegas   50
                         Shopping for Value   51
                         Timing Adds Value   53

Chapter Four:	Play the Game	55
	Step 1 – Check the Value Ratings	56
	Step 2 – Prepare a Score Sheet Using the Matchup Summary	57
	Step 3 – Check the Alignment Between the Value Rating and the Score Sheet	61
	Step 4 – Compare Your Predicted Point Spread to the Sports Book's Posted Point Spread	62
	Step 5 – Determine the Margin of Safety	63
	Check the Results	64
Chapter Five:	Get Ready for Next Week	67
	Updating NFL Value Ratings	67
	Use the Box Scores to Prepare a Score Sheet Analysis for Each Game Played	69
	It's Time for You to *Get In and Win*	70

1

Begin With the Basics

Imagine you're a pro football player standing in the tunnel before the start of the first game of the season. You're filled with excitement, eager to storm onto the field, hear the roaring crowd and get in the game. As you wait, you think about your preparation for this moment — countless hours of off-season workouts, suffering through never-ending training camp drills, studying endless reels of game film — all to get the edge you need to win against the toughest competition there is.

You're confident because you're prepared. You know that it's the precise execution of a solid game plan that produces winning results. The horn sounds, and you rush out in front of 70,000 screaming fans. That's probably the ultimate football fan fantasy: being part of the game.

While playing in the NFL isn't an option for must of us, we can still get in on the action. This *Get In and Win* Pro Football Playbook is your guide to predicting scores and game outcomes so you can get in on the action too with sports wagering.

I am not talking about placing a casual bet on your favorite team, but instead wagering in an intelligent, systematic manner, which means approaching sports betting in the same professional way that the best NFL players and coaches prepare for their games.

Proper Preparation

The first step is proper preparation. Instead of off-season workouts, you focus on key player and personnel changes across the NFL. Your training camp is reviewing and making the appropriate adjustments to the *Get In and Win* Value Ratings from the previous season. Studying endless reels of game film is replaced with analyzing the box scores from last season's games. This gives you the information you will need to get an edge over the other sports bettors.

As the season progresses, applying the proven *Get In and Win* analytical methods will deepen your understanding of the games. This will let you see the NFL through the eyes of the league's top players, coaches and general managers. Armed with the innovative and insightful *Get In and Win* perspective, you too can confidently step out of the tunnel and onto the field. It's game time!

The Fundamentals — a Review

Before you learn about preseason preparation and game-day wagering, we need to review three basic, fundamental elements of the *Get In and Win* System:

1. Value Ratings
2. Score Sheets
3. Matchup Summaries

Value Ratings

In a perfect world, a sports bettor is seeking one measurement that will tell him which team will win and which will lose, and by how much — one metric that is easy to understand, accurate and complete. The innovative *Get In and Win* Value Rating is that number. It is the one statistic you have been searching for. Carefully constructed and properly maintained, it can be a complete measure of a team's most likely actual performance. The *Get In and Win* Value Rating is the cornerstone of your handicapping process. This single number representing a team's overall strength can tell you more at a glance than reading multiple newspapers or spending countless hours combing the Internet, sifting through information that is of little or no value.

The benefit of using *Get In and Win's* Value Ratings as the core of your analysis is that they are objective arbiters of value. Value Ratings are unbiased, easy to understand, accurate and complete. When you use Value Ratings, the piles of individual and team statistics that bog down your game analysis suddenly disappear. Proper Value Ratings combined with your own knowledge and judgments are extremely accurate predictors of the outcomes of games. And as an added benefit, Value Ratings are an efficient way to correctly analyze a number of games in a short period of time.

The *Get In and Win* Value Ratings are an improvement over the familiar power rankings that can be found on every popular Internet website focused on sports (ESPN.com, SportingNews.com, FoxSports.com, CBSSports.com, etc.). Created just for sports betting, *Get In and Win's* own unique Value Rating is the next logical progression in terms of sophistication and simplicity.[1]

The Value Rating framework is based on my extensive research showing that team strength from top to bottom in all major sports can be quantified and remains constant from year to year. It is only the individual teams themselves that move around within the ranking system. The numerical rating for the best team, the second-best team, the third-best team and so on remains the same from year to year. The exercise then becomes determining which team is the best and which is the worst, and in what order the other teams fall in between.

In the NFL, there are 32 teams. After considerable mathematical modeling, we know that the best team in the league always plays to a Value Rating of 113 and the

---

[1] To determine the validity of new investment models, investment professionals often use a technique called "backtesting," which is a process that involves determining how reliably a new algorithm will likely perform using past data and Monte Carlo simulations. The *Get In and Win* Value Rating models are based on the extensively backtested work published by statisticians Jeff Sagarin and Kenneth Massey and verified by me.

worst team always plays to a Value Rating of 87. The Value Rating for an average team is 100.

This means that year in and year out (on a relative value basis), the best team in the NFL is approximately 26 points (113 - 87) better than the worst team. And the difference between the best team and an average team is 13 points (113 - 100). This same general Value Rating methodology holds true for the relationship between each of the other 30 teams in the NFL, meaning that there are 32 fixed positions on the Value Ratings scale for the NFL and it is only the teams that move around within those values from year to year and throughout the season. The Value Rating scale itself does not change.

Since the Value Rating framework for the NFL remains consistent from year to year, and because the Value Rating for each of the 32 positions within the framework has already been assigned,[2] your job is to determine the appropriate place on the rating scale for each team.

The Value Ratings at the end of the 2011–12 regular season are reported in Table 1.1:

---

[2] You will note that some of the positions have the same Value Rating. For example, the Value Rating for positions 4 and 5 is 108 and the Value Rating for positions 21, 22 and 23 is 96. So don't spend a lot of time determining if a team should be ranked 4 or 5, because in terms of betting value there is no difference; they are the same.

Table 1.1

GET IN AND WIN VALUE RATINGS
PRO FOOTBALL
DATE: January 24, 2012

RANK	VALUE RATING	TEAM
1	113	Green Bay Packers
2	110	New England Patriots
3	109	New York Giants
4	108	New Orleans Saints
5	108	Pittsburgh Steelers
6	107	San Francisco 49ers
7	106	Baltimore Ravens
8	105	Houston Texans
9	103	Detroit Lions
10	102	Atlanta Falcons
11	102	Cincinnati Bengals
12	101	Philadelphia Eagles
13	101	Dallas Cowboys
14	100	New York Jets
15	99	Miami Dolphins
16	99	San Diego Chargers
17	98	Seattle Seahawks
18	98	Tennessee Titans
19	97	Arizona Cardinals
20	97	Chicago Bears
21	96	Denver Broncos
22	96	Buffalo Bills
23	96	Carolina Panthers
24	95	Oakland Raiders
25	95	Washington Redskins
26	94	Kansas City Chiefs
27	94	Jacksonville Jaguars
28	93	Cleveland Browns
29	92	Minnesota Vikings
30	91	Tampa Bay Buccaneers
31	89	St. Louis Rams
32	87	Indianapolis Colts

LEARN HOW TO PREDICT PRO FOOTBALL SCORES!
Visit www.BookwormSports.com

For your use in developing your own set of Value Ratings, a blank *Get In and Win* Value Rating scale for the NFL is available at www.BookwormSports.com at no charge.

Score Sheets

The Score Sheet lets you drill into the detail and analyze the individual factors that determine the *score* of a game with just a few simple inputs. That's right, the Score Sheets provide a step-by-step method for forecasting the *total points* that each team will score in a game.

The Score Sheets are favorites of the fantasy sports fanatics. Using the Score Sheet, fantasy players can apply all the knowledge they have been accumulating over the years about their favorite players and teams to make a profit. Based on David Berri's and Martin Schmidt's sophisticated statistical and economic modeling techniques introduced in their best-selling book *The Wages of Wins*,[3] the easy-to-use Score Sheets are designed so you can plug in the relevant statistics and out pops an accurate prediction of the number of points each team will score.

And best of all, you don't have to do the regression arithmetic, because the Score Sheets do it for you. You simply use your knowledge of the teams and players to come up with the required inputs, and then work through a few simple computations to forecast the number of points each team will score.

To predict the number of points each team will score in an NFL game, you just need to make an informed estimate of the following seven items for each of the teams playing in the game:

- Rushing attempts
- Net rushing yards
- Passing attempts
- Net passing yards
- Fumbles
- Interceptions thrown
- Missed field goals

---

[3] Berri is a professor of economics at Southern Utah University, and Schmidt is a professor of economics at the College of William and Mary. They maintain a website, www.wagesofwins.com, and their writing on sports appears frequently in *The New York Times*.

Now, the fantasy players can get really detailed and use the estimated individual performances of each player to come up with the total for each category, but that is not really necessary. It's up to you to determine whether incorporating individual player performance improves your forecasting accuracy.

The economic theory behind allocating scarce, valuable investment capital forms the basis for the *Get In and Win* NFL Score Sheets, with offensive plays serving as the underlying currency and points earned being the economic measurement unit. Passing and rushing plays represent a *charge* or *use of capital*, with each passing play being assigned a negative value because the play consumes a resource (there are 63 offensive plays in the average NFL game — 36 passing plays[4] and 27 rushing plays). Because plays are limited in number, coaches should "spend" them carefully.

Moreover, a passing play can have an additional negative impact because the game clock stops on incomplete passes, which allows more time for the opposing team to possess the ball and provides additional opportunities for the opponent to score. Thus, passing plays *cost* a negative .33 points per play. On the other hand, while a rushing play also represents a *spent* play, the game clock usually continues to run after the rushing play is completed, which has the benefit of *reducing* the amount of time the opponent can possess the ball.

For rushing plays, the value received from keeping the game clock winding down more than compensates for the negative spending associated with using the play, so rushing plays have a positive value in the *Get In and Win* model. Thus, rushing plays are rewarded and are credited at a positive .07 points per play.

Since the basic purpose of rushing and passing plays is to advance the ball while attempting to score points, a point value can also be determined and assigned to each rushing yard and passing yard. Rushing yards have a value of .08 points per yard. Because more bad things can happen on a pass play (sack, interception, incompletion) than on a running play, pass plays are more risky, but when a pass is completed the average total yards gained are more than for the average running

---

4 In the *Get In and Win* System, sacks are considered passing plays.

play. Thus, pass plays are higher-risk but higher-reward and are assigned a value of .10 points per yard.

Table 1.2 summarizes the point values associated with running plays, passing plays and yards gained:

Table 1.2

	Rushing	Passing
Play Value	.07 points per play	-.33 points per play
Yardage Value	.08 points per yard	.10 points per yard

Finally, any experienced NFL fan can tell you that turnovers significantly influence game outcomes. Here's why: In the average NFL game, each team has approximately 12 scoring possessions, or *drives*, so each drive is extremely valuable. Every turnover committed (fumble and interception) or missed field goal uses up one of the 12 scoring opportunities with no points earned. To make matter worse, giveaways provide the opponent with an additional chance to score.

The *Get In and Win* Score Sheet values for turnovers and missed field goals are reported in Table 1.3:

Table 1.3

	Giveaways	Takeaways
Interceptions	-1.6 points	3.1 points
Fumbles	-2.1 points	1.9 points
Missed Field Goals	-4.2 points	N/A

For you use, a blank *Get In and Win* Pro Football Score Sheet is available at www.BookwormSports.com at no charge.

Matchup Analysis

Matchup Analysis is a method for evaluating team performance in specific areas of football compared to the performance of other NFL teams in those same areas. It is based on the mathematical concept of normal distribution developed by German mathematician Carl Friedrich Gauss, which says statistical data follow the pattern of a bell curve[5] as shown in Table 1.4 below:

Table 1.4

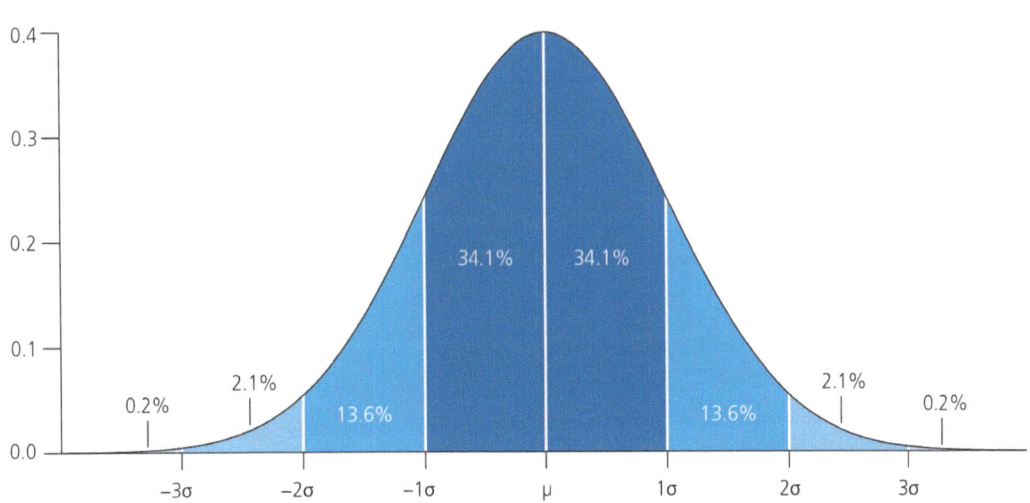

GET IN AND WIN THE BELL CURVE
PRO FOOTBALL

---

[5] It's called a bell curve because the chart is shaped like a bell.

When applied to NFL statistics, bell curve analysis tells us that we can group the performance of the 32 NFL teams into five distinct rating groups and rank the teams within the categories from best to worst. For the *Get In and Win* System, we call this a Matchup Analysis.

Table 1.5 shows the five team ratings (excellent, good, average, poor and awful), the percentage of the teams in each category, and what that means in terms of how many of the 32 NFL teams will be in each group. Moreover, to make the team ratings and Matchup Analysis simple to use and interpret, they are color coded using the "stoplight method"[6] where green represents excellent, light green represents good, yellow represents average, orange represents poor and red represents awful.

Table 1.5

GET IN AND WIN TEAM RATINGS
PRO FOOTBALL

CATEGORY	% OF TEAMS AT RATING	NUMBER OF TEAMS AT RATING
Excellent	2.3%	1 - 2
Good	13.6%	4 - 5
Average	68.2%	18 - 22
Poor	13.6%	4 - 5
Awful	2.3%	1 - 2

From the Score Sheets, we know that the seven most relevant statistics in determining the number of points a team will score are rushing attempts, net rushing yards, passing attempts, net passing yards, fumbles, interceptions thrown

---

6 It's called the "stoplight method" because it is similar to a stoplight, where green means go, yellow means use caution and red means stop.

and missed field goals. Using Table 1.5 we can see that for each of seven relevant game statistics (for example, rushing yards) there will be one or two NFL teams rated Excellent and one or two teams rated Awful. Moreover, there will be four or five teams rated Good and there will four or five teams rated Poor. And there will be 18 to 22 teams that are rated Average.

To determine the appropriate values for each of the relevant statistics, I performed a mean-variance calculation, and the results for rushing and passing are presented in the following tables.

Table 1.6

GET IN AND WIN RUSHING OFFENSE MATCHUP RATINGS
PRO FOOTBALL

CATEGORY	ATTEMPTS	YARDS	YARDS PER ATTEMPT
Excellent	>33.6	>155.9	>5.1
Good	30.4 - 33.6	135.2 - 155.9	4.6 - 5.1
Average	24.0 - 30.4	93.7 - 135.2	3.8 - 4.6
Poor	20.8 - 24.0	73.0 - 93.7	3.3 - 3.8
Awful	<20.8	<73.0	<3.3

Table 1.6 tells us that an excellent rushing team is one that runs the ball at least 34 times a game to gain more than 156 yards, or more than 5.1 yards per running attempt. On the other hand, the worst teams run the ball fewer than 21 times a game, gain less than 73 yards, and average less than 3.3 yards per carry. You can see for yourself what the numbers of the other rankings are.

Table 1.7

GET IN AND WIN PASSING OFFENSE MATCHUP RATINGS
PRO FOOTBALL

CATEGORY	ATTEMPTS	YARDS	YARDS PER ATTEMPT
Excellent	<29.2	>288.2	>7.5
Good	29.2 – 32.6	254.9 – 288.2	6.9 – 7.5
Average	32.6 – 39.3	188.3 – 254.9	5.5 – 6.9
Poor	39.3 - 42.6	155.0 – 188.3	4.8 – 5.5
Awful	>42.6	<155.0	<4.8

Table 1.7 shows that the best-passing teams throw the ball fewer than 29 times[7] a game, gaining in excess of 288.2 yards, and gain more than 7.5 yards per passing attempt. On the other hand, the worst-passing teams throw the ball more than 42 times a game while gaining less than 155 yards for a truly awful average of less than 4.8 yards per attempt.

Now let's look at the numbers for turnovers and field goals as presented in Table 1.8.

---

[7] The fact that the best-passing teams attempt fewer passes may seem counterintuitive to some. Recall from the Score Sheet that a passing play has a negative value of -.33 points per play. Thus, the more passing plays a team executes, the greater the number of yards that must be gained to offset the negative value associated with each play.

Table 1.8

GET IN AND WIN GIVE AWAYS AND MISSED FIELD GOALS MATCHUP RATINGS PRO FOOTBALL

CATEGORY	INTERCEPTIONS	FUMBLES	MISSED FGs
Excellent	< 0.3	< 0.2	< 0.0
Good	0.3 – 0.7	0.2 – 0.5	0.0 – 0.2
Average	0.7 – 1.3	0.5 – 0.9	0.2 – 0.5
Poor	1.3 – 1.7	0.9 -1.1	0.5 – 0.6
Awful	>1.7	>1.1	>0.6

Here we can see that for teams to be rated excellent in terms of minimizing turnovers or missing field goals, they need to throw, on average, fewer than .3 interceptions or have fewer than .2 fumbles or miss no field goals in a game. Awful teams, on average, throw more than 1.7 interceptions or have more than 1.1 fumbles or miss more than .6 field goals per game.

Next let's turn to the defensive half of the game. As presented in Table 1.9, Table 1.10 and Table 1.11, NFL team defenses can be rated in the same way as team offenses. While the defensive statistics are not used as inputs for the Score Sheet (only offensive statistics are used), the defensive statistics provide useful reference points for analyzing team performance and matchups between teams when forecasting the point spread for a game.

As an example, when a team with an excellent rushing offense plays a team with an awful rushing defense, it is likely (as well as obvious) that the excellent rushing team will have a high number of running plays and accumulate a significant amount of rushing yards. This information about NFL defenses is handy to have when preparing your Score Sheets for the games.

Table 1.9

GET IN AND WIN RUSHING DEFENSE MATCHUP RATINGS
PRO FOOTBALL

CATEGORY	ATTEMPTS	YARDS	YARDS PER ATTEMPT
Excellent	<20.8	<73.8	<3.3
Good	20.8 – 24.0	73.8 – 94.1	3.3 – 3.8
Average	24.0 – 30.4	94.1 – 134.8	3.8 – 4.6
Poor	30.4 – 33.5	134.8 – 155.1	4.6 – 5.0
Awful	>33.5	>155.1	<5.0

Table 1.10

GET IN AND WIN PASSING DEFENSE MATCHUP RATINGS
PRO FOOTBALL

CATEGORY	ATTEMPTS	YARDS	YARDS PER ATTEMPT
Excellent	>41.0	<177.1	<5.1
Good	38.5 – 41.0	177.1 – 199.3	5.1 – 5.6
Average	33.4 – 38.5	199.3 – 243.8	5.6 – 6.7
Poor	30.8 – 33.4	243.8 – 266.1	6.7 – 7.3
Awful	>30.8	>266.1	>7.3

Table 1.11

GET IN AND WIN TAKE AWAYS MATCHUP RATINGS
PRO FOOTBALL

CATEGORY	INTERCEPTIONS	FUMBLES
Excellent	>1.5	>1.1
Good	1.3 – 1.5	0.9 -1.1
Average	0.7 – 1.3	0.4 – 0.9
Poor	0.5 – 0.7	0.2 – 0.4
Awful	<0.5	<0.2

An old NFL axiom says, "Champions are made in the off-season." Similarly, it's your own preseason preparation that gets you ready to make accurate NFL score predictions and place winning sports bets when the season opens in September. So let's get started.

2

Preseason Preparation

It all begins in the preseason. The first step is to gather your primary research materials for the upcoming season. To supplement the information available on the well-known sports websites, I recommend purchasing Phil Steele's *Pro Football Preview* (www.PhilSteele.com) and *Football Outsiders Almanac* (www.footballoutsiders.com). With these in hand and access to the Internet, you're ready to begin your preseason analysis.

The Prior Year's Value Ratings Are the Starting Point

Begin with the prior season's ending Value Ratings. If you don't have Value Ratings from the prior season, you can develop your own by referencing the *Get In and Win* website (www.BookwormSports.com), Ken Massey's ratings (www.masseyratings.com) and Jeff Sagarin's ratings (www.sagarin.com).[8]

Prior Year Value Rating Adjustments

Next, you need to determine the appropriate adjustment that should be made to each team's prior-season-ending Value Rating by considering the following three factors that affect team performance from season to season:

---

[8] Jeff Sagarin provides ratings on sports teams to *USA Today* (since 1985), the NCAA basketball tournament selection committee (since 1984) and the Bowl Championship Series (since 1998). Kenneth Massey is a professor of mathematics at Carson-Newman College, and his college football team ratings have been a component of the Bowl Championship Series selection process since 1999.

1. Personnel changes (both players and coaches)
2. Team experience and player age
3. The influence of "luck" on the prior season's results
4. Teams that played fundamentally better or worse than their prior season win-loss record indicates

Obviously, changes in players and coaches can have a significant impact on team performance from year to year. Some teams get better because of personnel changes, and others get worse. Moreover, certain teams improve as their players gain more experience and benefit from the continuity of playing together while others decline as their players age. Based on your own knowledge and judgment, you will need to make a subjective assessment on whether to move a team up or down the Value Rating scale because of personnel changes, experience gains and age-related declines.

Determining the influence that "luck" or random events had on a team's performance in a prior season requires a more quantitative evaluation. In the NFL, luck shows itself in three ways:

1. Significant changes in a team's win-loss record, either up or down, from the prior season
2. Turnovers
3. Points scored or allowed that do not correlate with plays used and yards gained or allowed

The NFL's Law of Gravity

Several years ago, I came across an article written by Phil Steele, a well-respected football writer. In it, he described an eye-opening trend that he had observed during his many years analyzing professional and college football. Phil noted that teams that had significantly improved their record from one season to the next tended to reverse course and actually decline (some considerably) in year three.

What goes up …

As an example, in 2009, the Tampa Bay Buccaneers had a record of 3-13, followed by a 2010 record of 10-6 — a remarkable improvement of +7 wins. But in 2011, with expectations high, the Buccaneers posted a disappointing 4-12 record, or -6 wins when compared to 2010. Looking back further, consider the San Diego Chargers, who improved by +8 wins, going from 4-12 in 2003 to 12-4 in 2004, but slid back -3 wins to 9-7 in 2005. Also in 2004, the Pittsburgh Steelers logged nine more wins than they did in the prior season, improving from 6-10 in 2003 to 151 in 2004; but in 2005 their win total decreased by four as they fell back to 11-5.

Further research reveals that Tampa Bay's, San Diego's and Pittsburgh's fates were not anomalies. In fact, from 2002 to 2010, there were 76 NFL teams that increased their total wins by three or more games (+3 wins or more) from the season before.

often comes down …

You might be surprised to know that of these 76 teams that appeared to be showing significant improvement, only 11 were able to maintain an upward trajectory and post more wins in year three than in year two. As for the rest of the 76 teams, eight posted the same number of wins and a startling 57 teams had fewer wins. That means that 86 percent of the teams that appeared to be rising dynasties turned into disappointments.

Here are the nine teams that had three or more wins in 2011–12 than in 2010–11 and could disappoint in 2012–13.

Tabl.e 2.1

2012–13 Teams Most Likely to Disappoint?

Team	
San Francisco	+ 7 wins
Cincinnati	+ 5 wins
Green Bay	+ 5 wins
Carolina	+ 4 wins
Denver	+ 4 wins
Detroit	+ 4 wins
Houston	+ 4 wins
Arizona	+ 3 wins
Tennessee	+ 3 wins

Don't Despair, It Will Get Better

Even more interesting is that this trend analysis works just as well in reverse. Steele reports that since 2002 there have been 64 teams that have had four or more[9] losses than they had in the previous year and 47 (73 percent) had a better record the next year. For teams that declined by six or more losses, Steele's research shows that 21 out of 23 (91 percent) had an improved record in the third year.

In 2011–12, there were eight teams with four more losses in 2010–11 than in 2009–2010, and five of those teams improved their records. At the top of the list were the Cincinnati Bengals and the Carolina Panthers. The Bengals improved by five wins, going from 4-12 in 2010 to 9-7 in 2011, which was good enough to earn a spot in the playoffs. The Panthers jumped up four games from a woeful 2-14 in 2010 to 6-10 in 2011. However, the flip side of this good news is that both teams are now on the likely decliners list for 2012–13 because both improved by more than three games over the prior season. Nevertheless, the Bengals and Panthers fans enter this season with high expectations because of their significant turnarounds.

Table 2.2 presents the teams that had at least four more losses in 2011–12 than they did in 2010–11 and are poised to rebound in the upcoming season.

Table 2.2

2012–13 Teams Most Likely to Improve?

Team	
Indianapolis	+ 8 losses
Tampa Bay	+ 6 losses
St. Louis	+ 5 losses

---

9 This is in contrast to three or more wins for improving teams.

Takeaways and Turnarounds

As every football fan knows, turnovers have a huge impact on games and on a team's season. As an example of the importance that turnovers have on game outcomes, consider Super Bowl XXVII, played between the Dallas Cowboys and the Buffalo Bills. In that game, the Bills had the dubious distinction of committing nine turnovers, which stills stands as the record for the most turnovers recorded in an NFL playoff game. The Bills' inability to take care of the football resulted in a lopsided 52-17 win for the Cowboys.

Another startling example of the significance of turnovers occurred in a 2002 game when the Pittsburgh Steelers hosted the Houston Texans. The Texans (a first-season expansion team) were so outgained, so overwhelmed, so inept offensively, that they couldn't get anything right on offense. The Texans quarterback, David Carr, was under such pressure that he practically quit throwing the ball. Their running game barely produced a yard per carry. Yet in a game of numbers so one-sided that they are rarely seen in the NFL — the Steelers had 422 total yards and the Texans had 47 — the most remarkable was on the scoreboard, which showed a 24-6 rout. However, shockingly, it was the Texans that won the game. No NFL team had ever played as badly as the Texans. How could this happen? The deciding factor in the game was turnovers: five for Pittsburgh and one for Houston. Ouch!

Turnovers not only make a big difference in a game, they can also make the difference between a winning season and a losing one. At the end of the season, the best teams always recover more fumbles and get more interceptions than the worst ones. The difference between the number of turnovers won versus. the number lost is called the takeaway ratio; a positive ratio is a good thing. The more positive the ratio, the more games a team is likely to win.

For the 2011–12 season, the teams that had the highest takeaway ratios also had the league's best records. San Francisco had the highest takeaway ratio at +28.[10] The 49ers finished the season with a record of 13-3, were the NFC West champions,

---

10 For 2011–12, San Francisco intercepted 22 of their opponents' passes and recovered 16 of their opponents' fumbles, which resulted in 38 total takeaways by the 49ers. Conversely, their opponents picked off five of San Francisco's passes and recovered five of San Francisco's fumbles,

and advanced in the playoffs to the NFC championship game, where they lost in overtime to the eventual Super Bowl champion, New York Giants. Following San Francisco, the Green Bay Packers had the second-highest takeaway ratio at +24. In 2011–12, the Packers had the NFL's best record at 15-1 and won the NFC North. Their season came to an abrupt end when they too lost to the New York Giants in the divisional round of the playoffs. The New England Patriots had the third-best takeaway ratio at +17 in 2011–12. For the season the Patriots posted an AFC-best record of 13-3, won the AFC East and advanced to the Super Bowl, only to lose to the New York Giants in a game where the Patriots had one turnover[11] and the Giants had none.

What few sports fans know is that the takeaway ratio is also a significant indicator of how the team will do the following year, but just as in the Pittsburgh-Houston game, it may not be in the way you might assume.

In addition to the research Phil Steele has performed with regard to teams that significantly improve or decline from the previous year, he has also developed some very interesting stats and facts related to turnovers. Steele found that for teams that have a very high takeaway ratio in one season, there is approximately a 75 percent chance they won't win as many games the following year. However, if they had a very negative ratio one season, there is a 70 percent chance they will have a better win-loss record the next year.

Since 1991, there have been a total of 70 NFL teams with a +12 takeaway ratio. Of those teams, 51 (73 percent) had worse records the following year. Moreover, from 2005 to 2011 there were 19 teams with a +12 ratio; 17 of them did worse the following season. Out of these 70 teams with a +12 ratio, eight had the same record the next year and only 11 (16 percent) were able to improve their record the next season.

Here are some examples of teams with high takeaway ratios and how they performed the following year:

---

which produced 10 giveaways for the 49ers. Subtracting 38 takeaways from 10 giveaways results in a +28 takeaway ratio.
11 A Tom Brady interception.

- In 2008–09, Miami was +17 in turnovers and the Dolphins went from 11-5 in 2008–09 to just 7-9 in 2009–10.

- Tennessee had a +14 takeaway ratio in 2008–09 and finished the season 13-3. In 2009–10, the Titans did not catch the same breaks and they dropped to 8-8.

- Baltimore went 11-5 in 2008–09 and made an appearance in the AFC Champ game thanks in large part to being +13 in turnovers. The next year, the Ravens did not have the same good fortune and fell to 9-7.

On the other hand, if a team receives some bad breaks the year before, it will usually be fortunate the following year. Since 1991, 70 NFL teams suffered from -12 turnovers or more.[12] Of those teams, an amazing 48 (69 percent) had a better record the next season and eight had the same. Only 14 (20 percent) did not improve their record the next season.

As an example of a team that had a significantly negative turnover ratio, consider the 1996 New York Jets, who were a league-low -20 and finished the season with a record of 1-15. The next season, disciplinarian Bill Parcells arrived and the Jets improved to +3 and finished with a winning record of 9-7. Now, that's a real Takeaways and Turnarounds story!

Table 2.3 presents a ranking of all 32 NFL teams by their takeaway ratio for 2011–12. It shows the teams that are most likely to improve their overall win-loss record and which teams are most likely to decline. The results will probably surprise you.

---

[12] The fact that the number of teams since 1991 with a +12 takeaway ratio or a -12 takeaway ratio is the same (70) is consistent with the mathematical principle of normal distribution and the bell curve that was introduced in Chapter One.

Table 2.3

GET IN AND WIN TAKE AWAY RATIO
PRO FOOTBALL
Teams Likely to Win More Games and Teams Likely to Win Less Games
SEASON: 2011 – 2012

TEAM		
SAN FRANCISCO	+ 28	GOING DOWN
GREEN BAY	+ 24	GOING DOWN
NEW ENGLAND	+ 17	GOING DOWN
Detroit	+ 11	
Seattle	+ 8	
Atlanta	+ 8	
New York Giants	+ 7	
Houston	+ 7	
Jacksonville	+ 5	
Dallas	+ 4	
Chicago	+ 2	
Baltimore	+ 2	
Carolina	+ 1	
Tennessee	+ 1	
Buffalo	+ 1	
Cleveland	+ 1	
Cincinnati	0	
Kansas City	- 2	
Minnesota	- 3	
New Orleans	- 3	
New York Jets	- 3	
Oakland	- 4	
St. Louis	- 5	
Miami	- 6	
San Diego	- 7	
DENVER	- 12	GOING UP
INDIANAPOLIS	- 12	GOING UP
ARIZONA	- 13	GOING UP
PITTSBURGH	- 13	GOING UP
PHILADELPHIA	- 14	GOING UP
WASHINGTON	- 14	GOING UP
TAMPA BAY	- 16	GOING UP

When preparing your Value Ratings for the upcoming season, remember to consider the takeaway ratio, because big numbers, either positive or negative, can lead to big turnarounds in a team's win-loss record.

Score Sheets Show the Lucky, Unlucky and Overrated, and Teams on the Rise

Another way to determine the effect that "luck" had on points scored and a team's performance in a prior season is to perform a Score Sheet analysis using the past season's statistics.

The Lucky of 2011–12

As an example, consider the Green Bay Packers' performance during the 2011–12 season. Score Sheet 2.4 presents an analysis of the Packers' 2011–12 performance using actual average game statistics.

Score Sheet 2.4

GET IN AND WIN SCORE SHEET 2.4
PRO FOOTBALL
TEAM: GREEN BAY PACKERS
SEASON: 2011 – 2012 (Average per Game)

	FACTOR VALUE		OFFENSE	PLAY AVG	DEFENSE	PLAY AVG
RUSHING						
Play Cost	0.07	Rushing Plays	24.7		23.9	
Yardage Value	0.08	Yards	97.4	3.9	111.8	4.7
		Rushing Points	9.5		10.6	
PASSING						
Play Cost	-0.33	Passing Plays	37.0		41.6	
Yardage Value	0.10	Yards	307.0	8.3	299.8	7.2
		Passing Points	18.5		16.3	
GIVE AWAYS		**GIVE AWAYS**				
Interceptions	-1.6	Interceptions	0.5		1.9	
Fumbles	-2.1	Fumbles	0.4		0.4	
Missed FG's	-4.2	Missed FG's	0.3		0.3	
		Give Away Points	-2.9		-5.1	
TAKE AWAYS		**TAKE AWAYS**				
Interceptions	3.1	Interceptions	1.9		0.5	
Fumbles	1.9	Fumbles	0.4		0.4	
		Take Away Points	6.7		2.3	
SCORE PREDICTION			31.8		24.0	
ACTUAL POINTS			35.0		22.4	
DIFFERENCE			-3.2		-1.6	

LEARN HOW TO PREDICT PRO FOOTBALL SCORES USING THIS SCORE SHEET!
Visit www.BookwormSports.com for your copy of *Get In and Win Quick Start*

From this we see that the Packers should have scored, on average, 31.8 points per game and allowed 24 points per game. The Packers actually scored 35 points per game and allowed 22.4 points per game. The Packers' on-the-field performance was better than the Score Sheet analysis would have expected by 4.8 points. This indicates luck had a positive impact on the Packers' team performance.

Table 2.5 presents a review of the Packers' 2011–12 performance in the key offensive and defensive areas using the *Get In and Win* Matchup analysis tables presented in Chapter One.

Table 2.5

	GET IN AND WIN MATCHUP RATINGS
	PRO FOOTBALL
	TEAM: PACKERS
	SEASON: 2011 – 2012

STATISTIC	OFFENSE	DEFENSE
Rushing Attempts	Average	Good
Rushing Yards	Average	Average
Rushing Yds/Att	Average	Poor
Passing Attempts	Average	Excellent
Passing Yards	Excellent	Awful
Passing Yds/Att	Excellent	Poor
Interceptions	Good	Excellent
Fumbles	Good	Poor
Field Goals	Average	N/A

So now we can tell that while the Packers were an excellent passing team and a poor defensive team, it was their ability to minimize their own turnovers and pick off a lot of their opponents' passes that caused them to be successful.[13]

For 2011, the Packers had an NFL-best record of 15-1 and outscored their opponents by a total point differential of 201 points per game (12.6 points per game). The Score Sheet analysis confirms a significant positive turnover ratio was a primary factor in the Packers' margin of victory. Moreover, our Score Sheet analysis shows that the Packers actually scored 3.2 points per game and allowed 1.6 points per game more than the statistics indicate they should have.

What does all this mean?

First, even if we reduce the Packers' per-game margin of victory by 4.8 points, it probably wouldn't have had much impact on their 2011–12 record; they would have still outscored opponents by more than a touchdown (8 points per game instead of

---

[13] It also helps to explain why the Giants were able to defeat the Packers in the 2012 Divisional Round of the playoffs when Green Bay lost three fumbles and Eli Manning passed for 66 more yards than Aaron Rodgers (Manning: 330 yards; Rodgers: 264 yards).

12.8). In other words, they still would have won most of their games by more than a touchdown and an extra point.

Second, it is highly unlikely that the Packers will be able to maintain that significant turnover edge by picking off as many passes in 2012 as they were able to in 2011. Thus, when establishing your 2012–13 Value Ratings for Green Bay, it would be reasonable to consider a reduction, possibly a significant one, to the Packers' 2011–12 final Value Rating.

Let's look at another team that was also in the lucky group for 2011–12, the New Orleans Saints. For the 2011–12 season, the Saints had a record of 13-3 and scored 208 points more than their opponents did (13 points per game). However, their actual points scored and allowed were 5.3 points better than their statistics would indicate.

Score Sheet 2.6

GET IN AND WIN SCORE SHEET 2.6
PRO FOOTBALL

TEAM: NEW ORLEANS SAINTS

SEASON: 2011 – 2012 (Average per Game)

	FACTOR VALUE		OFFENSE	PLAY AVG	DEFENSE	PLAY AVG
RUSHING						
Play Cost	0.07	Rushing Plays	26.9		21.9	
Yardage Vaue	0.08	Yards	132.9	4.9	108.6	5.0
		Rushing Points	12.5		10.2	
PASSING						
Play Cost	-0.33	Passing Plays	42.9		41.2	
Yardage Value	0.10	Yards	334.2	7.8	259.8	6.3
		Passing Points	19.3		12.4	
GIVE AWAYS		**GIVE AWAYS**				
Interceptions	-1.6	Interceptions	0.9		0.6	
Fumbles	-2.1	Fumbles	0.3		0.4	
Missed FG's	-4.2	Missed FG's	0.4		0.3	
		Give Away Points	-3.8		-3.1	
TAKE AWAYS		**TAKE AWAYS**				
Interceptions	3.1	Interceptions	0.6		0.9	
Fumbles	1.9	Fumbles	0.4		0.3	
		Take Away Points	2.6		3.4	
SCORE PREDICTION			30.6		22.9	
ACTUAL POINTS			34.2		21.2	
DIFFERENCE			-3.6		-1.7	

LEARN HOW TO PREDICT PRO FOOTBALL SCORES USING THIS SCORE SHEET!
Visit www.BookwormSports.com for your copy of *Get In and Win Quick Start*

Score Sheet 2.6 shows that the Saints actually scored 3.6 more points per game and allowed 1.7 fewer point per game than the statistics indicate.[14] They should have scored, on average, 30.6 points per game and allowed 22.9 points per game.

Now let's look at how the Saints ranked in the key performance areas:

Table 2.7

GET IN AND WIN MATCHUP RATINGS
PRO FOOTBALL
TEAM: SAINTS
SEASON: 2011 – 2012

STATISTIC	OFFENSE	DEFENSE
Rushing Attempts	Average	Good
Rushing Yards	Average	Average
Rushing Yds/Att	Good	Awful
Passing Attempts	Awful	Excellent
Passing Yards	Excellent	Poor
Passing Yds/Att	Excellent	Average
Interceptions	Average	Poor
Fumbles	Good	Poor
Field Goals	Average	N/A

The *Get In and Win* Matchup Analysis presented in Table 2.7 shows that the Saints used a high-risk, high-reward strategy in 2011–12. While New Orleans had a high number of passing attempts, their All-Pro quarterback, Drew Brees, was exceptionally productive as measured by total passing yards and yards per attempt. Thus, the Saints were an excellent passing team and their running game was good (as measured in yards per attempt).

---

14 This may explain the Saints' early exit from the 2011–12 playoffs (despite being favored by more 7.5 points over the San Francisco 49ers) when Drew Brees threw two interceptions and the Saints defense allowed the 49ers to gain an incredible 6.5 yards per rushing attempt.

The Saints used their outstanding offense to take the pressure off a defense that was subpar. To cover up for a defense that was awful against the run (as measured by yards per attempt) and poor against the pass (in passing yards allowed), New Orleans used a fast-paced offensive strategy that forced their opponents to abandon the run and pass the ball to keep up with Drew Brees's high-scoring offense or risk falling far behind.

What does all this mean?

While reducing the Saints per-game margin of victory by 5.3 points (as Score Sheet 2.3 indicates) would not to appear to have had a significant impact on the Saints' 2011–12 record (they would still have outscored their opponents by 7.7 points instead of 13 points), it seems reasonable to assume that the Saints would not have been as effective in dictating the game tempo if their scoring opportunities were reduced. Thus, when establishing your 2011–12 Value Ratings, it would seem reasonable to make a significant reduction to the Saints' 2010–11 ending Value Rating.[15]

The Unlucky of 2011–12

Now, let's look at an unlucky team from the 2011–12 season, the World Champion New York Giants. You might ask, "How can the team that won the Super Bowl be considered unlucky?" An analysis of the Giants' 2011–12 regular season performance shows that they played much better than their regular season record of 9–7 would indicate, which goes a long way toward explaining why they did so well in the postseason, eventually winning the Super Bowl.

According to Score Sheet 2.8, the Giants should have won their games by an average of 4.8 points per game.

---

15 Considering that the Saints' head coach, Sean Payton, defensive coordinator, Greg Williams, and several key players have been suspended for all or part of the 2012–13 season, adjusting the their 2012–13 Value Rating for luck is probably of little consequence.

Score Sheet 2.8

GET IN AND WIN SCORE SHEET 2.8
PRO FOOTBALL
TEAM: NEW YORK GIANTS
SEASON: 2011 – 2012 (Average per Game)

	FACTOR VALUE		OFFENSE	PLAY AVG	DEFENSE	PLAY AVG
RUSHING						
Play Cost	0.07	Rushing Plays	25.7		27.2	
Yardage Value	0.08	Yards	89.2	3.5	121.3	4.5
		Rushing Points	8.9		11.6	
PASSING						
Play Cost	-0.33	Passing Plays	38.6		39.8	
Yardage Value	0.10	Yards	295.9	7.7	255.1	6.4
		Passing Points	16.9		12.4	
GIVE AWAYS		**GIVE AWAYS**				
Interceptions	-1.6	Interceptions	1.0		1.3	
Fumbles	-2.1	Fumbles	0.5		0.7	
Missed FG's	-4.2	Missed FG's	0.3		0.4	
		Give Away Points	-3.9		-5.2	
TAKE AWAYS		**TAKE AWAYS**				
Interceptions	3.1	Interceptions	1.3		1.0	
Fumbles	1.9	Fumbles	0.7		0.5	
		Take Away Points	5.4		4.1	
SCORE PREDICTION			27.2		22.8	
ACTUAL POINTS			24.6		25.0	
DIFFERENCE			+2.6		+2.2	

LEARN HOW TO PREDICT PRO FOOTBALL SCORES USING THIS SCORE SHEET!

Instead, we see that, on average, they lost by .4 points per game. Turning a .4-point-per-game scoring disadvantage into a 4.8-point advantage would have had a HUGE effect on the Giant's regular season record. They should have scored, on average, 27.2 points per game and allowed 22.8 points per game. That's a difference from their actual results of almost a touchdown (without the extra point) per game. If that had happened, the Giants would have won a lot more games during the regular season. This shows that the Giants were a victim of some bad luck.

Here's where New York ranked in our key performance areas:

Table 2.9

GET IN AND WIN **MATCHUP RATINGS**
PRO FOOTBALL
TEAM: GIANTS
SEASON: 2011 – 2012

STATISTIC	OFFENSE	DEFENSE
Rushing Attempts	Average	Average
Rushing Yards	Poor	Average
Rushing Yds/Att	Poor	Average
Passing Attempts	Average	Good
Passing Yards	Excellent	Poor
Passing Yds/Att	Excellent	Average
Interceptions	Average	Good
Fumbles	Average	Average
Field Goals	Average	N/A

What does all this mean? Table 2.9 reports that except for their passing attack led by Eli Manning and Victor Cruz, the Giants were fundamentally an average team. Thus, when establishing your 2012–13 Value Ratings, it would seem reasonable to rank the Giants higher than their 2011–12 regular season Value Rating, but probably not at the top of scale as you might expect for a Super Bowl champion.

The Overrated of 2011–12

Score Sheet 2.10 shows that the 2011–12 New England Patriots were an overrated team.

Score Sheet 2.10

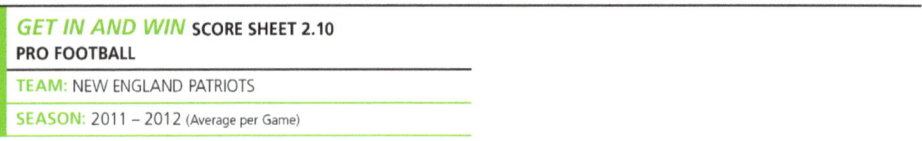

	FACTOR VALUE		OFFENSE PLAY AVG		DEFENSE PLAY AVG	
RUSHING						
Play Cost	0.07	Rushing Plays	27.4		25.3	
Yardage Vaue	0.08	Yards	110.3	4.0	117.1	4.6
		Rushing Points	10.7		11.1	
PASSING						
Play Cost	-0.33	Passing Plays	40.3		41.2	
Yardage Value	0.10	Yards	317.8	7.9	293.9	7.1
		Passing Points	18.5		15.8	
GIVE AWAYS		**GIVE AWAYS**				
Interceptions	-1.6	Interceptions	0.8		1.4	
Fumbles	-2.1	Fumbles	0.3		0.7	
Missed FG's	-4.2	Missed FG's	0.3		0.2	
		Give Away Points	-3.2		-4.6	
TAKE AWAYS		**TAKE AWAYS**				
Interceptions	3.1	Interceptions	1.4		0.8	
Fumbles	1.9	Fumbles	0.7		0.3	
		Take Away Points	5.7		3.0	
SCORE PREDICTION			31.7		25.4	
ACTUAL POINTS			32.1		21.4	
DIFFERENCE			-0.4		-4.0	

LEARN HOW TO PREDICT PRO FOOTBALL SCORES USING THIS SCORE SHEET!

From this, we see that the Patriots' actual points scored were in line with the points they should have scored. However, their defense's actual on-the-field performance was better than the Score Sheet analysis would have predicted by 4 points per game. This indicates that the Patriots were not fundamentally as good as their 2011–12 regular season record indicates.

A Matchup Analysis showing the Patriots' performance in our key offensive and defensive areas is reported in Table 2.11.

Table 2.11

GET IN AND WIN MATCHUP RATINGS
PRO FOOTBALL
TEAM: PATRIOTS
SEASON: 2011 – 2012

STATISTIC	OFFENSE	DEFENSE
Rushing Attempts	Average	Average
Rushing Yards	Average	Average
Rushing Yds/Att	Average	Average / Poor
Passing Attempts	Poor	Excellent
Passing Yards	Excellent	Awful
Passing Yds/Att	Excellent	Poor
Interceptions	Average	Good
Fumbles	Average	Average
Field Goals	Average	N/A

From Table 2.11, we can tell that the excellent play of the Patriots' All-Pro quarterback, Tom Brady, covered serious deficiencies on the defensive side of the ball. Their rushing defense had issues as indicated by their borderline poor yards-per-attempt rating. Against the pass, the Patriots were awful, allowing more passing yards per game than any other team in the NFL. It was only their high interception rating that saved their defense from being abysmal.

What does all this mean?

With Brady at the controls, the 2011–12 Patriots were still an explosive team. But if the defense had not been the beneficiary of some good fortune, then the Patriots' average margin of victory would have been reduced from almost 11 points per game to fewer than 7 points per game. Moreover, considering that the high interception rate also contributed significantly to propping up the defense, it's obvious that the 2011–12 Patriots were a very good team, but not as dominant as their record and actual margin of victory would indicate.

When determining the appropriate 2012–13 Value Rating for the Patriots, think about whether or not the fact that the Patriots used their top six selections (two in the first round) in the NFL draft to pick defensive players will be enough to shore up a defense desperately in need of improvement.

2011–12's Team on the Rise

Finally, we'll look at a team that performed well in 2011–12 and might very well be on the rise, the Houston Texans. While the Texans finished the 2011–12 season with a 10-6 record and won the AFC South, a review of their fundamental performance shows that they could have done even better.[16]

According to Score Sheet 2.12 analysis, the Texans should have scored 2.8 points more per game and allowed their opponents to score 2.6 points less per game than they did.

---

16 The late season injury to their star quarterback, Matt Schaub, probably explains a lot of the Texans' underperformance.

Score Sheet 2.12

GET IN AND WIN SCORE SHEET 2.12
PRO FOOTBALL
TEAM: HOUSTON TEXANS
SEASON: 2011 – 2012 (Average per Game)

	FACTOR VALUE		OFFENSE PLAY AVG		DEFENSE PLAY AVG	
RUSHING						
Play Cost	0.07	Rushing Plays	34.1		23.6	
Yardage Value	0.08	Yards	153.0	4.5	96.0	4.1
		Rushing Points	14.6		9.3	
PASSING						
Play Cost	-0.33	Passing Plays	381.3		36.4	
Yardage Value	0.10	Yards	219.1	7.7	189.7	5.2
		Passing Points	11.6		7.0	
GIVE AWAYS		**GIVE AWAYS**				
Interceptions	-1.6	Interceptions	0.6		1.1	
Fumbles	-2.1	Fumbles	0.7		0.6	
Missed FG's	-4.2	Missed FG's	0.4		0.4	
		Give Away Points	-4.1		-4.7	
TAKE AWAYS		**TAKE AWAYS**				
Interceptions	3.1	Interceptions	1.1		0.6	
Fumbles	1.9	Fumbles	0.6		0.7	
		Take Away Points	4.6		3.2	
SCORE PREDICTION			26.6		14.8	
ACTUAL POINTS			23.8		17.4	
DIFFERENCE			+2.8		+2.6	

LEARN HOW TO PREDICT PRO FOOTBALL SCORES USING THIS SCORE SHEET!
Visit www.BookwormSports.com for your copy of *Get In and Win Quick Start*

This means that the Texans underperformed by a whopping 5.4 points less per game than their actual play indicated. If the Texans had not had some bad luck and had performed in accordance with their statistics, they would have outscored their opponents by 11.8 points per game.

Recall from Score Sheet 2.4 that the Green Bay Packers had the best record in the NFL in 2011–12 and outscored their opponents by 12.6 points per game. Thus, when considering fundamental performance, the Texans played at almost the same outstanding level as the Packers did on the field.

How did the Texans do it? Table 2.13 shows how the Texans ranked in the *Get In and Win* Matchup Analysis.

Table 2.13

GET IN AND WIN MATCHUP RATINGS
PRO FOOTBALL
TEAM: TEXANS
SEASON: 2011 – 2012

STATISTIC	OFFENSE	DEFENSE
Rushing Attempts	Excellent	Good
Rushing Yards	Good	Average
Rushing Yds/Att	Average	Average
Passing Attempts	Good	Average
Passing Yards	Average	Good
Passing Yds/Att	Good	Good
Interceptions	Good	Average
Fumbles	Average	Average
Field Goals	Average	N/A

From the Matchup Analysis, it's obvious that the 2011–12 Texans were good in all aspects of the game, making them a solid all-around team.[17] Drilling down even further and referring to Score Sheet 2.10, we see that, as measured in terms of points per game, the Texans held the advantage over their opponents in the following key performance areas:

---

17 It's too bad that Matt Schaub, the Texans' starting quarterback, and Matt Lienart, his backup, were both injured, forcing a rookie, T.J. Yates, to direct the team for five regular season and two playoff games.

- Rushing Offense: 5.3-points-per-game advantage (14.6 points compared to 9.3 points);

- Passing Offense: 4.6-points-per-game advantage (11.6 points compared to 7 points);

- Giveaways: 0.6- point-per-game advantage (-4.1 points compared to -4.7 points);

- Takeaways: 1.4-points-per-game advantage (4.6 points compared to 3.2 points).

Based on their overall performance in 2011–12, it would seem obvious to move the Texans up on your *Get In and Win* Value Rating scale for 2012–13, especially with a healthy Matt Schaub back under center. Exactly how far up to move them on the scale is up to your own judgment.

Run the Numbers From the Prior Season

To achieve optimal results, the *Get In and Win* System integrates both a top-down (Value Ratings) and bottom-up approach (Score Sheets) for predicting the point spread for each game. As part of your preseason preparation, you will need to rank the teams on the *Get In and Win* Value Rating scale and develop the inputs you will be using for your score-prediction Score Sheets when the season opens. The best way to come up with a team's early-season Value Rating as well as an estimate for each of their early-season key performance statistics is to prepare a Score Sheet and Matchup Analysis recapping their 2011–12 performance.[18]

Previously, we discussed how to create and interpret a historical Score Sheet and Matchup Analysis for several teams that revealed their strengths and weaknesses.[19] To estimate the value for the key performance statistics for the upcoming season,

---

[18] There are 32 NFL teams, so you will need to prepare 32 Score Sheets and 32 Matchup Analyses.
[19] Specifically, we reviewed the 2011–12 performance of the Green Bay Packers, the New Orleans Saints, the New York Giants, the New England Patriots and the Houston Texans.

simply adjust the previous season's performance numbers up or down based on your judgment of any changes the team has made that you think will affect the way they will play during the upcoming season.

For example, during the 2012 off-season, the Dallas Cowboys signed free agent cornerback Brandon Carr to a $50.1 million contract and moved up to claim cornerback Morris Claiborne with the sixth overall pick in the NFL draft. Will this overhaul at the cornerback position improve Dallas's pass defense? Will the change result in more interceptions by the Cowboys' defense? If so, how many?

Recall that there are only three key Score Sheet statistics that these expensive changes in the Cowboys' secondary could directly impact: opponent's passing attempts, opponent's passing yards and interceptions. So in the final analysis, these two much-publicized signings will add value only if there is significant improvement in these key areas. And best of all, using the *Get In and Win* Score Sheet you can make your own estimate of the points-per-game value that Carr and Claiborne will add to determine, based on your own judgment, if it's enough to help Dallas make a deep playoff run.[20]

As another example, consider the Denver Broncos' off-season signing of free agent quarterback Peyton Manning. How will his addition impact the Broncos in the key performance areas? Can he perform at an All-Pro level? Will his play dramatically increase Denver's offensive production, and might it also indirectly benefit the Broncos defense by taking some pressure off of that unit?

These are challenging, interesting and fun questions to consider, and *Get In and Win* provides you with a proven framework to make these evaluations as you get ready for the new season along with your favorite teams, players and coaches. After using *Get In and Win*, you will have an entirely new way to think about and enjoy the NFL. Keep reading and you will discover that having fun can be profitable too.

---

20 The Cowboys have one playoff win since 1996.

Read the Board

Sports books have to cram a lot of information into a limited amount of space. To save "real estate" on the board, they post only the numbers and assume you know what they mean.

This picture is from a typical Las Vegas casino-based sports book:

Consider the first game on the upper left, which looks like this:

Oct. 11, 2009 — Vikings Vs. Rams			
401	Vikings	-10	-600
402	Rams	41	+400

- 401 and 402 are the rotation numbers. These are just the numbers sports books give to each team or participant in a game or match. Every sports book uses the same rotation numbers for each game, so the rotation numbers for the Vikings and Rams game is the same at all Las Vegas casinos and across the Internet. This makes a lot of things easier, and helped avoid confusing your bet on the Arizona Cardinals with your bet on the St. Louis Cardinals.
- -10 is the point spread. This is for point-spread wagers.
- 41 is the total points expected to be scored. This is for use in total bets.
- +400 and -600 are money lines. These are used in money line bets.

Point spreads, totals and money lines are the standard types of bets offered by sports books.

- **Point-Spread Bets:** A point-spread bet is a standard wager for or against the point spread. For point spread-bets, the bettor must generally risk $11 to win $10.
- **Total Bets:** Total bets are similar to point-spread bets, except the bettor bets on the total points scored. In the example above, the wager is whether the total points combined between the Vikings and Rams will be over or under 41. Like point-spread bets, the bettor must generally risk $11 to win $10.
- **Money Line Bets:** Money line bets are simply wagers on who will win straight up, without considering the point spread. The number represents the odds associated with each team's winning or losing the game. In the example above, +400 for the Rams means that a $100 bet on the Rams would win $400 if the Rams win the game. The money line on the Vikings is -600, which means that the bettor must risk $600 to win $100.

The most common type of sports betting proposition is the point-spread wager. In this example, the Vikings are favored to win by 10 points, so two point-spread bets would be available on this game: (1) that the Vikings will win by 11 or more points; or (2) that the Rams win, or lose by 9 or fewer points. If the Vikings win by exactly 10, then point-spread bets on both sides would "push," meaning there is no winner or loser and the amount wagered is returned to the bettors.

Usually the point spread is displayed next to the favored team and is thus expressed as a negative number.[21] The point spread is also referred to as *the line*. Each sports book sets a point spread in a way that will best balance betting on both sides of the point spread and maximize betting action — not to reflect the likely outcome of the game.

The point spread can be viewed as a handicap given to the team favored to win the game. Therefore, when you wager on a favorite, you're giving (or "laying") points. When you bet on an underdog, you're taking or receiving points. The point spread theoretically makes any game an equal proposition on the sports betting market, no matter how great the actual mismatch between the two teams might seem to be. The purpose of the point spread is to equally divide the amount of money wagered on the game, so that the amount bet on the Vikings is the same as the amount bet on the Rams.

A slight variation on the point spread is the half point. This means adding or subtracting a half point from a whole number. For example, -7 points in our example might be changed to -6.5 or -7.5. The half point, commonly referred to as the hook, was devised to eliminate pushes and convert them to wins or losses.

Why Lines Move: Not All Point Spreads Are Equal

Shopping for the best available line or quote is another way to make more winning wagers. Every sports book sets its point spreads differently and changes its lines based on circumstances. This difference in pricing between the sports books provides an additional opportunity to add value to the bets you're placing.

---

21 Some not familiar with sports betting find it counterintuitive that the team with negative number next to its name (in this instance the Vikings) is the team the sports betting public expects to win the game. If you're one of those that find this confusing, simply remember to subtract the number of "minus points" from the favored team's final score to determine the winner of the wager.

Remember that sports books make their money by withholding a commission on winning wagers. So they do have a small vested interest in the outcome of every game. For the sports books, the ideal is a perfectly balanced line where the money taken from the losers goes to the winners, and the house gets to pocket its service charge from all the winners. In the real world, the betting action is rarely perfectly balanced. When wagering action isn't balanced, the sports book is in danger of paying out more than it takes in. This is when the sports book is exposed. Each sports book determines how exposed it can be on any given event. A combination of its own tolerance for risk and the wagering activity is what drives line changes.

Sports books that move lines too far can suffer heavy losses, as will sports books that don't move lines enough. The difficulty in knowing when to move lines is what makes line-making an art and not a science. Just know that every sports book moves its lines a little differently, so every day there are differences between the lines posted at different sports books for the exact same game. The differences among the books provide you, the value-seeking bettor, with an opportunity to do some bargain shopping and make your wager at the best price.

Off-Standard Point Spreads

Sports books also use off-standard point spreads to balance the betting on an event. Recall that the standard payoff on an NFL point spread is 10/11 (or -110), where the bettor must risk $11 to win $10, but occasionally sports books deviate from that. Anything other than -110 is referred to as an "off-standard" line, and it happens a lot in football. The reason is because football is unique among the major pro sports in terms of how points are scored.

Football is complicated because the scoring comes in chunks of 3 and 7 points. There are also other scoring possibilities, with safeties scoring 2 points, missed extra points making a touchdown worth only 6, and the 2-point conversion making 8 a possibility, but they are less likely combinations.

What's more, in football, scoring tends to take place an average of only about eight times a game and, as a result of few scores, the final scores do group around certain numbers, known as "key numbers." The **major key numbers are 3 and 7**, but 1, 4, 6, 10, 13 and 14 also have a high likelihood of being the final margin of victory and are sometimes referred to as **minor key numbers**.

If we look at how all these numbers relate to 3 and 7, it's easy to see why they occur frequently. Table 3.1 shows the frequency of certain final game margins for the NFL, as well as the relationship between the number of points and a combination of touchdowns and field goals:

Table 3.1

Game Margin	Frequency	Combinations
3 points	16.0%	Field Goal
7 points	11.3%	Touchdown
6 points	6.6%	Two Field Goals
10 points	5.1%	Touchdown and Field Goal

In order to balance wagering activity without moving on or off key numbers, sports books alter the odds associated with the point spread. For example, the sports books might offer the game at -120, meaning you must risk $120 to win $100. So when sports books move a point spread, the odds don't change, as the spreads only affect whether your wager is a winner or not. Changing the odds, on the other hand, doesn't affect whether your wager is a winner or not, but instead affects the payout. By changing the odds away from the standard of -110, the sports books can make the same point spread more or less attractive to the bettors.

Betting on Totals: A Simple Path to Success

There is no simpler wager to understand than the game total. Simply add the score of the two teams together, and if it is higher than the posted total, the *over* wins. If it is lower than the posted number, the *under* wins.

With totals, you don't need to worry about which team is better. All you need to know is how the game will be played. To calculate the total number of points each team is predicted to score, use the Score Sheet. It doesn't get easier than that.

When wagering on NFL totals, always be sure to check the weather. Sports books take weather into account, and so should you. Rain and snow aren't as important factors as many people make them out to be, since defenders are just as likely to slip as offensive players and one or two big plays can drive a total way up. Wind, on the other hand, is underrated (in my opinion) and forces teams to run more. This can eat up the clock and help lower total scores.

Totals are a very important part of a bettor's arsenal. Spend time looking through the totals of all the games and you can find some betting opportunities.

Money Lines: It's Not As Hard as You Think

Most bettors favor point spreads over money lines, simply because point spreads are easier to understand. With point spreads, it's easy to spot the difference between -3 and -4, right? But how much value is there between money lines of -170 and -210? Most people don't get that; it's just not intuitive to most bettors. Bettors like point spreads because there isn't a lot of math involved and they seem less intimidating. However, the math for the money line is actually much easier than most people realize.

Here is a quick primer:

To start with, reading a money line is very simple. A typical money line would look something like this:

> Denver Broncos -160
> Miami Dolphins +140

The -160 means you must risk $160 to win $100 on the Broncos, while the +140 means you get back $140 for each $100 risked should the Dolphins win outright.

Any minus number means the amount that is put at risk to win $100, and any plus number is the payoff for risking $100. It's that simple. In the event of a tie, all money line wagers are settled as a push, and bets are refunded.

The difference between the two lines is described in "cents." In football, it typically starts at 20 cents and gets larger as the numbers get higher. For example, if the favorite is -240, the underdog may be +200, a difference of 40 cents. The higher difference at higher numbers simply serves to keep the commission for the sports book roughly the same as a percentage of the amount wagered.

Thus there is a question you need to ask yourself about every single game you bet on: Is there more value in the point spread or the money line? The answer to that question is based on your assessment of two things:

Is this team likely to win but not cover?

Is this team likely to cover but not win?

Now let's compare a spread to a money line. Although each sports book is different, Table 3.2 presents the chart that most sports books use as a guideline for converting point spreads to money lines for the NFL. You can use it to convert your own point spreads for NFL games, calculated using the Value Rating and Score Sheet methods into money lines.

Moreover, Table 3.2 allows you to compare the point spread to the money line to see if there is an inconsistency that could provide sports betting value.

Table 3.2

NFL POINT SPREAD TO MONEY LINE CONVERSION CHART

Favorite Point Spread	Corresponding Money Line
-2	-130/+110
-2.5	-140/+120
-3	-155/+135
-3.5	-175/+155
-4	-200/+170
-4.5	-220/+180
-5/-5.5	-240/+190
-6	-270/+210
-6.5	-300/+220
-7	-330/+250
-7.5/-8/-8.5	-360/+280
-9/-9.5	-400/+300
-10	-450/+325
-11	-550/+375
-12	-600/+400
-13	-650/+450

NFL money lines aren't traditionally offered for point spreads outside the 2–14 range because at those extremes it becomes difficult for sports books to balance the betting action. If a spread moves from -1.5 to -1, they don't have much room to move on the money line. Players will simply ignore betting the +1 and take the underdog at +105 or even, lowering the commission for the sports book. Above 14, the money lines are just too high. Bettors seldom take the big price, and the sports book exposes itself to a significant loss when big upsets happen.

Money line bets are covered in detail in the *Get In and Win* Specialty Plays Playbook.

Proposition Bets

Most sports books provide bettors with an opportunity to make bets that are not directly related to the outcome of a game. These bets are known as proposition wagers and are commonly called *props* or *prop bets*. Prop bets are based on the odds associated with how many times a particular event — sacks, field goals or pass completions, for example — will occur during a game. If you're involved in fantasy sports, many prop bets offer a way to profit on the research you're already doing for your fantasy team. Fantasy players do so much research on individual players that being able to wager on individual players holds a lot of appeal.

Prop bets are usually determined individually by each sports book, so they will not always be the same from one book to the next. While all props are unique among sports books, once you begin analyzing them you will find that each book consistently offers many of the same prop bets week after week to its own customers as a way to keep them coming back. Because most books usually release dozens of props every day, there is a good chance you will find some that provide solid betting value.

The most popular event for sports books in terms of props is the Super Bowl. While there are hundreds of props for the Super Bowl, many of them are too frivolous for the serious bettor. But prop bets are also offered throughout the rest of the NFL season. Typical football prop bets include total passing yards by a quarterback, total number of sacks by one or both teams, rushing yards by a particular player, number of field goals by a kicker and number of catches by a receiver.

The following is an example of a common proposition wager:

Green Bay Packers vs. Detroit Lions

Total Number of QB Sacks in the Game

Over +170 *o*

6

Under -210 *u*

In the example above, the +170 *o* means a $100 bet on the Packers and the Lions combining for more than six quarterback sacks (the *o* is for over) would win $170. The over bet would be a winner if the Packer and Lions combine for seven sacks or more in the game. On the other hand, -210 *u* means the bettor must risk $210 to win $100. The under bet would a winner if the Packers and Lions combine for five or fewer sacks (the *u* is for under) in the game. If the teams combine for exactly six sacks, then the wager is a push and the bettor gets his money back.

Proposition bets are covered in detail in the *Get In and Win* Specialty Plays Playbook.

Sports Books: The Internet vs. Las Vegas

Now that you know about how point spreads are set and changed as well as the common betting opportunities, let's look at the different types of sports books and how you can best take advantage of them.

A land-based book is one in which you have to be present in order to place a bet. In the United States, most of the legally licensed land-based sports books are in Las Vegas. There, bettors stand in line, cash in hand, at sports betting counters waiting to place their wagers with sports book employees. This limits the number of wagers that you can place at any point in time. Conversely, Internet books can process thousands of transactions simultaneously. Since it is not necessary to have a person handle every wager, Internet books have much lower cost structures. These cost advantages are *sometimes* passed along to bettors in the form of lower commission charges.

Las Vegas sports books also suffer some geographical influence. Their clients are predominantly from California, Nevada, Arizona and other nearby states. Many of those clients bet on their favorite teams, and the hometown bias tends to drive up the price on West Coast teams. Internet sports books can suffer from the same issue if their marketing is heavy in one city or state, but since comparisons are very easy to do over the Internet, those biases don't last long. Thoughtful players looking for an edge move in to take advantage of the values they see in the online point spreads, which in turn causes the Internet line quotes to become more balanced between all the Internet sports books.

Imagine being in Las Vegas and trying to go from the Mirage to Bally's, from Bally's to the Bellagio and then to Mandalay Bay so that you could check the posted lines. It would take hours. By the time you realized the original line at the Mirage was the best, the odds would have probably changed! With your computer, on the other hand, you can check the lines at dozens of Internet sports books in mere seconds. You don't have to drive through traffic, pay for parking (or taxis), walk through the casino maze, and then wait in line to place a wager. With Internet sports books, you can compare lines very quickly and act almost instantly when you see a line you like.

The Internet makes it very easy to get the best odds on any game. Regardless, it is illegal to make a sports bet from your computer if you are located anywhere in the United States, including Nevada. As a respected financial advisor, I personally do not make illegal wagers and am not advising you to do so. That's why if you are a U.S. citizen and plan to wager legally using the information in this guide, you will need to go to a location where sports betting is allowed.

While there are a lot of advantages to sports betting online, Las Vegas books will always have a place in the market. Sitting in a comfortable room with hundreds of other sports fans, tracking all the point spreads, watching dozens of TVs, drinking ice cold beer and eating 99-cent hot dogs is just too much fun to be completely replaced by the online experience.

Shopping for Value

If you have an account at only one sports book, you have no choice but to either accept the line offered or not bet. If you use two sports books, you can compare the lines offered and wager on the one that provides you with the best opportunity to win. In an NFL matchup between Dallas and Washington, why would you wager Dallas at -7.5 if you could have made the same wager on Dallas with another sports book at -7?

Estimates vary, but getting an extra half point can increase your chance of winning a wager by about 4 percent.[22] You can imagine the compounding effect of getting an extra half point or full point on every bet over the course of a full season.

This is particularly important around the key numbers in football, 3 and 7, and smaller point spreads in other sports. In other words, it is more likely that the difference between a 2-point and a 2.5-point line is going to be of more significance than the difference between a 22-point and a 22.5-point line. But it doesn't mean you shouldn't make an effort to get the best line possible every time.

As an example, we can look at an imaginary NFL football game between the Pittsburgh Steelers and the Kansas City Chiefs. There can be times when the lines quoted by various sports books might range from the Steelers -9 to -10.5. If Pittsburgh wins by a final score of 26-16, which sports book you chose would make a big difference as to whether you will be cashing a winning ticket or taking a loss.

It's up to you to decide how many sports books you should use. Too few means you probably won't have enough variation in the lines quoted. On the other hand, having too many may cause you to lose some opportunities because it might take too long to shop all the lines and your sports betting capital could be spread too thin.

Be sure to choose sports books where it is easy to access the features you need very quickly. The *USA Today* website (www.usatoday.com) provides a side-by-side comparison of the lines quoted by some of the most popular sports books. Any of the sports books on the *USA Today* website would be good additions to your lineup of wagering alternatives.

The magic number is probably five sports books. But if you have only one account, just adding another sports book to get one more set of line quotes could make a big difference to your bottom-line profits at the end of the season. A half point can turn a loss into a push or a push into a win. Getting a few extra wins or pushes over the course of the season makes that extra shopping well worth the effort.

---

22 Derived from *Sports Book Management – A Guide for the Legal Bookmaker*.

Timing Adds Value

Another factor in beating the point spread and boosting your Win Rate is timing. Sometimes the morning paper says the point spread is Cowboys -6.5, but by the time you go to bet, the point spread is -5.5.

Paying close attention to opening lines and then monitoring how the point spread moves before placing a bet can add value. For example, if a line opens at -6.5 and moves to -6, you know sports books are getting action on the underdog. If you like the favorite in that particular game, you may be better served by waiting as the point spread moves from -6 to -5.5 to -5 over the course of the day or the week.

This is tougher to do than shopping for the best line and takes some experience to get a feel for which way point spreads move. But after a couple of weeks of tracking opening and closing lines, you will be well prepared to get the best possible number on your wagers.

As a starting point, experienced bettors use the following guideline for shopping NFL point spreads. Generally the public prefers favorites (and so-called overs when it comes to total score bets, meaning a bet that the total points scored will be over the amount listed by the sports book), so the lines tend to move in that direction (but not always, or sports books would simply raise their opening lines).

Thus the rule of thumb is to play favorites and overs early and underdogs and unders late. You won't get the absolute best point spread every time by following this guideline, but it should serve as a solid base and will boost your Win Rate.

Play the Game

It's time to get down to it and play the game. Combining both a "top-down" and "bottom-up" approach, the *Get In and Win* System incorporates two original and proprietary methods for your use when calculating your own forecasted point spread: the Value Rating and the Score Sheet.

The Value Rating uses a top-down approach that assigns a relative value to each team and then ranks each team on a predetermined scale. The Score Sheet is a bottom-up analysis of the factors influencing the actual performance of each specific team.

The power of these methods is in their ease of use. Even though each of the methods is based on some very sophisticated mathematics, the *Get In and Win* System has simplified their application so that anyone can use them.

The steps for successful NFL wagering are summarized below:

- **Step 1** – Develop a set of Value Ratings to get an objective assessment of the strength of each team and to predict the point-spread differential between teams.
- **Step 2** – Prepare a Score Sheet using the Matchup Analysis to project the score of a specific game using your best estimate of certain game statistics. With

the Score Sheet's projection of the number of points each team is expected to score in hand, you have another tool to establish a point spread for a game.

➢ <u>Step 3</u> – To set your own final forecast for the point spread, apply your own knowledge and judgment to align the Value Rating and Score Sheet projections for the point spread.

➢ <u>Step 4</u> – Compare your forecasted point spread for the game to the sports book's posted point spread.

➢ <u>Step 5</u> – Determine if an adequate Margin of Safety exists between your forecasted line and the sports book's posted line. If the Margin of Safety is reasonable, place your wager. If it is unsatisfactory, pass and move on to analyzing the next bet.

STEP 1 – Check the Value Ratings

To make predictions for upcoming games, simply compare the ratings for the teams and add 3 points to the home team's Value Rating to reflect the statistically significant home field advantage.

As an example, let's look at Super Bowl XLVI, played between the New England Patriots and the New York Giants, using our season-ending Value Ratings. The point spread for the game was:

Giants *u* 53

Patriots -3

Let's see how you would have used the *Get In and Win* Value Ratings, presented in Table 1.1, to predict the score of Super Bowl XLVI. As of January 24, 2012, New England was rated at 110 and New York was rated at 109. Since the Super Bowl was played at a neutral site[23], there is no home team adjustment. In other NFL games, 3 points are added to the home team's Value Rating.[24] Let's do the math: 110 minus

---

23 The game was played at Lucas Oil Stadium in Indianapolis, Indiana.
24 See Chapter Five of my book *Changing the Game: How to Profit From Your Passion for Sports* for a detailed example of how to adjust the home team's Value Rating.

109 equals 1. Therefore, you would expect New England to win the game by 1 point.

It's that easy — take the Value Rating for each team from your *Get In and Win* Value Ratings ranking scale, adjust for home field advantage, and then compare the Value Rating for each of the teams playing in the game. Presto, you have your own point spread for the outcome of the game. Thus, for the 2012 Super Bowl, the *Get In and Win* Value Rating point spread would have been New England -1.

STEP 2 – Prepare a Score Sheet Using Matchup Analysis

Next, use the Score Sheet to forecast a likely margin of victory for the game. To begin, start with a Matchup Analysis detailing the strengths and weaknesses of each team's offense and defense. Following along with the Patriots-Giants example, here are the Matchup Analyses for the Super Bowl.

Table 4.1

GET IN AND WIN **MATCHUP ANALYSIS**
PRO FOOTBALL
TEAM: PATRIOTS OFFENSE vs. GIANTS DEFENSE

STATISTIC	PATRIOTS OFFENSE	GIANTS DEFENSE
Rushing Attempts	Average	Average
Rushing Yards	Average	Average
Rushing Yds/Att	Average	Average
Passing Attempts	Poor	Good
Passing Yards	Excellent	Poor
Passing Yds/Att	Excellent	Average
Interceptions	Average	Good
Fumbles	Average	Average
Field Goals	Average	N/A

Table 4.2

GET IN AND WIN MATCHUP ANALYSIS
PRO FOOTBALL
TEAM: GIANTS OFFENSE vs. PATRIOTS DEFENSE

STATISTIC	GIANTS OFFENSE	PATRIOTS DEFENSE
Rushing Attempts	Average	Average
Rushing Yards	Poor	Average
Rushing Yds/Att	Poor	Average / Poor
Passing Attempts	Average	Excellent
Passing Yards	Excellent	Awful
Passing Yds/Att	Excellent	Poor
Interceptions	Average	Good
Fumbles	Average	Average
Field Goals	Average	N/A

So we see that while New England and New York match up about the same in rushing offense and defense (both are hovering around average), it's New York that has an advantage in the passing game. That's because both Tom Brady and Eli Manning are the leaders of excellent passing attacks but New England's very weak pass defense gives the Giants the advantage. In terms of turnovers, New England and New York match up about the same, with both teams being good at intercepting their opponents' passes.

Next let's complete a Score Sheet to predict the score of the game, taking into account New England's and New York's performance in the key statistical areas using the Matchup Analyses presented in Tables 4.1 and 4.2 while also considering any adjustments that might be necessary based on the strengths and weaknesses of each team.

There is no mechanical formula for making the appropriate adjustments and estimating the key statistics to use in the Score Sheet. The adjustments and estimates are based on your unique sports knowledge, judgment and experience. Therefore, the advantage in sports wagering, as well as in NFL football,[25] goes to the more skilled, better prepared and properly disciplined player.

---

[25] It's also knowledge, judgment and discipline that give the experienced investor an advantage on Wall Street.

Score Sheet 4.3

GET IN AND WIN SCORE SHEET
PRO FOOTBALL
GAME: Super Bowl XLVI
DATE: February 5, 2012

				Visitor **GIANTS**		Home **PATRIOTS**	
	FACTOR VALUE			PLAY AVG		PLAY AVG	
RUSHING							
Play Cost	0.07		Rushing Plays	27.0		24.0	
Yardage Value	0.08		Yards	105.0	3.9	105.0	4.4
			Rushing Points	10.3		10.1	
PASSING							
Play Cost	-0.33		Passing Plays	38.0		42.0	
Yardage Value	0.10		Yards	300.0	7.9	260.0	6.2
			Passing Points	17.5		12.1	
GIVE AWAYS			**GIVE AWAYS**				
Interceptions	-1.6		Interceptions	1.0		1.0	
Fumbles	-2.1		Fumbles				
Missed FG's	-4.2		Missed FG's				
			Give Away Points	-1.6		-1.6	
TAKE AWAYS			**TAKE AWAYS**				
Interceptions	3.1		Interceptions	1.0		1.0	
Fumbles	1.9		Fumbles				
			Take Away Points	3.1		3.1	
SCORE PREDICTION				**29.3**		**23.7**	

LEARN HOW TO PREDICT PRO FOOTBALL SCORES USING THIS SCORE SHEET!
Visit www.BookwormSports.com for your copy of *Get In and Win Quick Start*

Score Sheet 4.3 forecasts that the Giants will defeat the Patriots by the score of 29.3-23.7, which is a 5.6-point margin. Let's review the key assumptions used in Score Sheet 4.3:

- **Number of Plays:** During the 2011–12 season, the Patriots averaged 68 offensive plays and the Giants averaged approximately 64 offensive plays.[26] Since they rely on the pass, the Patriots play an up-tempo game, whereas the Giants are a bit more balanced between running and passing, so they average fewer plays. Score Sheet 4.3 assumes the Giants have 65 offensive plays and the Patriots have 66.

- **Rushing offense:** The Matchup Analyses presented in Tables 4.2 and 4.3 indicate that both teams rate about average in overall rushing offense. While the estimates for the rushing statistics in Score Sheet 4.3 put both teams in the average range for all the inputs, it reflects the fact that the Giants run the ball a few more times a game than the Patriots but are less successful in terms of yards per attempt. Score Sheet 4.3 reports that the Giants have a .2-point advantage in rushing, reflecting the boost the Giants receive from controlling the clock[27] despite rushing for fewer yards per attempt.

- **Passing offense:** This is the aspect of the game that will decide whether the Patriots or the Giants will win Super Bowl XLVI and by how much. Tables 4.2 and 4.3 show that both passing offenses are excellent but the Giants defense has the advantage (over the Patriots defense) in terms of total yards allowed and, more importantly, in yards allowed per attempt. Since the Patriots rank awful in both passing yards allowed and passing yards allowed per attempt, it's reasonable to assume that Eli Manning will continue his excellent performance against the vulnerable Patriots secondary. While the Patriots' passing attack is probably just as potent as the Giants', the Giants' pass defense has performed better. Thus, it's reasonable to assume that Brady will have a good day but his results will not match Manning's. Score Sheet 4.3 reports that the Giants have a 5.4-point advantage in passing offense.

- Giveaways: Since both teams pass a lot and are good at picking off their opponents' passes, it's sensible to forecast that each team will get one interception, which results in no advantage for either team in the Giveaways or Takeaways categories.

---

26 Recall from Chapter One that the NFL average is 63 offensive plays per game.

27 Recall from Chapter One that rushing plays have a positive value because the value received from keeping the game clock winding down more than compensates for the negative spending associated with using the play.

STEP 3 – Check the Alignment Between the Value Rating and the Score Sheet

You have now calculated your own point spread for the game in two ways. The first used Value Ratings and the second used the Score Sheet method. Recall that Value Ratings provide a broad-brush or top-down view of the strength of each team. The Value Rating summarizes a lot of information in a single number and is heavily influenced by a team's actual performance. On the other hand, the Score Sheet provides its own special perspective by looking at a game from a bottom-up, fundamental view, considering the statistics that are most relevant in determining points scored.

What you're seeking is alignment between the results of both methods. You will rarely have an exact match, but you need them to be in balance. Remember that what you are looking for is a substantial difference between the sports book's posted point spread and your predicted outcome of the game. Alignment gives you the confidence to act decisively when you spot that difference.

If your point-spread prediction using Value Ratings is not comparable to your Score Sheet calculation, you should carefully examine your inputs and assumptions for each. That way you're constantly testing and refining your opinions about the capabilities of each team as you try to bring the Value Ratings and Score Sheets into alignment. While *Get In and Win* provides you with a reliable valuation framework to get an edge, it is ultimately your own knowledge and judgment that will determine whether there is alignment between the Value Rating predictions and your Score Sheet forecasts.

If after careful consideration you're unable to get them in balance for a particular game and you don't believe additional adjustments are called for, don't despair — just don't bet. In my book *Changing the Game*, you learned there are no called strikes in sports wagering, so the only way you can make an out is to swing and miss. When there is no alignment, pass and move on, because placing a bet when you don't have an edge increases your chances of striking out.

Continuing with the Patriots-Giants Super Bowl example, there is "directional" alignment between the Value Rating and the Score Sheet when compared to the posted point spread. The Value Rating shows that the Patriots should be favored by 1 point and the Score Sheet forecasts a 5.6-point New York victory over New England.

While at first glance this may seem like a large difference, a closer examination reveals a welcome result. Recall that the posted point spread for the game is the Patriots -3. At the Patriots -3, both our Value Rating point spread (which is the Patriots -1) and our Score Sheet point spread (which is the Giants -5.6) show the posted line being in favor of the Giants. Moreover, from Score Sheet 2.8,[28] we know that the 2011–12 Giants were an unlucky team that fundamentally played better than the results indicated. On the other hand, Score Sheet 2.10,[29] shows that the Patriots' results in 2011–12 were better than they should have been given their very shaky pass defense. Thus, it would be sensible to adjust the predicted point spread more in the direction of the fundamentally based Score Sheet forecast. In this instance, since 3 is a key number in pro football,[30] we will set our predicted point spread for Super Bowl XLVI at Giants -3.

As this example shows, the process of bringing the Value Rating's and Score Sheet's predicted point spread into alignment often requires several iterations as well as considerable knowledge and judgment.

STEP 4 – Compare Your Predicted Point Spread to the Sports Book's Posted Point Spread

Next we compare our forecast of the point spread to the sports book's posted point spread to determine if there is a substantial difference between our forecast and the posted point spread. In this example, the sports book's posted line says the Patriots are favored by 3 points. But our forecast predicts that the Giants will win by 3 points. That means there is a 6-point difference between the sport book's posted point spread and our prediction. This difference indicates that the Patriots are overvalued by the betting public and the Giants are undervalued.

---

[28] See Chapter Two.
[29] See Chapter Two.
[30] See Table 3.1.

STEP 5 – Determine the Margin of Safety

Now we are ready to examine where the real money is made. Recall, as discussed extensively in *Changing the Game*, that the posted line is not the sports book's prediction for the game. The posted line only represents the point spread necessary to evenly divide the wagering action and allow the sports book to balance its books.

The difference between your calculated point spread and the posted line is called the Margin of Safety — and the bigger the difference, the larger the Margin of Safety. You should bet only when there is a comfortable Margin of Safety. The appropriate Margin of Safety is tricky to assess and is a function of your overall judgment as an Intelligent Bettor. While there is no exact numerical threshold for determining a suitable Margin of Safety, my experience on Wall Street tells me that you want at least a 15 percent Margin of Safety in order to place a wager and risk your precious capital.

So for the Patriots-Giants game, the key question becomes: Is the Margin of Safety related to this 6-point difference large enough to place a wager on the Giants?

Table 4.5, at the back of this chapter, presents the Pro Football Margin of Safety Cheat Sheet. This chart is very important because it is used to determine the Margin of Safety for all NFL games. Looking at it, we find that the Margin of Safety between our forecasted point spread of the Giants -3 and the posted line of New England -3 is 37 percent (look down the -3 column and across the +3 row and you will find the number 37 in the box where the specified row and column meet).

This means that New York can play 37 percent worse than our forecast before we lose the bet. Another way to look at it is that New York can absorb a number of unanticipated negative factors such as injuries, turnovers, bad bounces, lucky plays, etc., before we lose our bet on the Giants. Since a 37 percent Margin of Safety is greater than our 15 percent threshold requirement, a bet on the Giants is a high-value bet, meaning we should place a wager on the underdog Giants.

Check the Results

In this instance, a wager on the Giants would have also been a winning bet, because the Giants won Super Bowl XLVI, 21-17.

Moreover, most sports books posted the *total* wager for the game at 53. So if we had bet the *under*, then we would have had two winning wagers: one on the point spread and the other on the total. However, our prediction for the score of the game as calculated in Score Sheet 4.3 had the Giants winning 29.3-23.7. Thus, our forecast for the total points scored was 53, which was exactly the same as the posted total. That means there was no value or Margin of Safety in the total wager, so the appropriate play would have been to pass and not bet on the total.

Let's do a quick Score Sheet review of the actual results from the game to see how the

Giants were able to win.

Score Sheet 4.4

GET IN AND WIN SCORE SHEET
PRO FOOTBALL

GAME: Super Bowl XLVI
DATE: February 5, 2012

	FACTOR VALUE		Visitor GIANTS		Home PATRIOTS	
			PLAY AVG		PLAY AVG	
RUSHING						
Play Cost	0.07	Rushing Plays	26.0		19.0	
Yardage Value	0.08	Yards	114.0	4.4	83.0	4.4
		Rushing Points	10.9		8.0	
PASSING						
Play Cost	-0.33	Passing Plays	43.0		43.0	
Yardage Value	0.10	Yards	282.0	6.6	266.0	6.2
		Passing Points	14.0		12.4	
GIVE AWAYS		**GIVE AWAYS**				
Interceptions	-1.6	Interceptions	0.0		1.0	
Fumbles	-2.1	Fumbles	0.0		0.0	
Missed FG's	-4.2	Missed FG's	0.0		0.0	
		Give Away Points	-0.0		-1.6	
TAKE AWAYS		**TAKE AWAYS**				
Interceptions	3.1	Interceptions	1.0		0.0	
Fumbles	1.9	Fumbles	0.0		0.0	
		Take Away Points	3.1		0.0	
SCORE PREDICTION			28.1		18.8	
ACTUAL SCORE			21.0		17.0	

LEARN HOW TO PREDICT PRO FOOTBALL SCORES USING THIS SCORE SHEET!
Visit www.BookwormSports.com for your copy of *Get In and Win Quick Start*

Score Sheet 4.4 shows that the Giants played even better than the results on the scoreboard indicated. While they won the game by 4 points, the Score Sheet analysis of the game reveals that the Giants played at a level that was approximately 10 points better than the Patriots. That's dominance!

How did they do it?

First, the Giants were better in the running game than the Patriots, giving them a 2.9-point advantage. As predicted, the Giants' passing attack was able to successfully exploit the Patriots' woeful secondary, but Brady was able to hold his own through the air, with the Giants gaining only a 1.6-point advantage in the passing game.

However, the Giants were able to force Brady into throwing one interception, while Manning didn't make a mistake, and that was the big difference, resulting in a 4.6-point swing in the takeaway/giveaway aspect of the game. So in the final analysis, Brady's pick was what made the difference.

Table 4.5

GET IN AND WIN MARGIN OF SAFETY CHEAT SHEET (% DIFFERENCE)
PRO FOOTBALL

CHART A — PREDICTED LINE (columns); POSTED LINE (rows)

	-2.0	-2.5	-3.0	-3.5	-4.0	-4.5	-5.0	-6.0	-6.5	-7.0	-8.0	-9.0	-10.0	-11.0	-12.0	-13.0
-2.0		3	8	10	15	18	20	23	25	27	28	29	31	33	34	35
-2.5	3		5	7	13	15	17	20	22	24	26	27	29	31	32	33
-3.0	9	5		2	8	10	13	16	18	20	21	23	25	27	28	29
-3.5	12	8	2		6	8	11	14	16	18	20	21	23	26	27	27
-4.0	18	14	8	6		3	5	9	11	13	15	17	18	21	22	23
-4.5	22	18	12	9	3		3	6	8	11	12	14	16	19	20	21
-5.0	25	21	15	12	6	3		3	6	8	10	12	14	17	18	19
-6.0	29	25	19	16	9	6	4		3	5	7	9	11	14	15	16
-6.5	33	29	22	19	12	9	6	3		3	4	6	8	11	13	13
-7.0	36	32	25	22	15	12	9	5	3		2	4	6	9	10	11
-8.0	39	34	27	24	17	14	11	7	4	2		2	4	8	9	10
-9.0	42	37	30	27	20	16	13	10	7	4	2		2	5	7	8
-10.0	45	40	33	30	23	19	16	12	9	6	5	2		3	5	6
-11.0	50	45	38	34	27	23	20	16	13	10	8	6	3		1	2
-12.0	52	47	39	36	29	25	22	17	14	11	10	7	5	1		1
-13.0	53	49	41	38	30	26	23	19	16	13	11	8	6	2	1	

CHART B — PREDICTED LINE (columns); POSTED LINE (rows)

	-2.0	-2.5	-3.0	-3.5	-4.0	-4.5	-5.0	-6.0	-6.5	-7.0	-8.0	-9.0	-10.0	-11.0	-12.0	-13.0
2.0	23	25	29	31	35	37	38	40	42	44	44	46	47	49	49	50
2.5	26	28	32	34	37	39	41	43	44	46	47	48	49	51	51	52
3.0	32	34	37	39	42	44	45	47	49	50	51	52	53	55	55	56
3.5	35	37	40	41	45	46	48	49	51	52	53	54	55	56	57	57
4.0	41	43	46	47	50	52	53	54	56	57	57	58	59	61	61	62
4.5	45	46	49	50	53	54	56	57	58	59	60	61	62	63	63	64
5.0	48	49	52	53	56	57	58	60	61	62	62	63	64	65	66	66
6.0	52	54	56	57	60	61	62	63	64	65	66	66	67	68	69	69
7.0	56	57	59	60	63	64	65	66	67	68	68	69	69	70	71	71
8.0	59	61	63	63	66	67	67	68	69	70	71	71	72	73	73	73
9.0	62	63	65	65	67	68	69	70	71	72	72	73	73	74	75	75
10.0	65	66	67	68	70	71	72	73	73	74	74	75	76	76	77	77
11.0	68	69	70	71	73	74	74	75	76	76	77	77	78	79	79	79
12.0	73	74	75	76	77	78	78	79	79	80	80	81	81	82	82	82
13.0	75	75	77	77	79	79	80	80	81	81	82	82	83	83	83	84
14.0	76	77	78	79	80	81	81	82	82	83	83	83	84	84	84	85

5

Get Ready for Next Week

Imagine it's Sunday evening or Monday morning and all the week's games, except for Monday Night Football, have been played. The highlight shows are flashing on the flat screens and the box scores recapping the game results are on the Internet and in the newspapers.

What do you do? To keep the fun and profits rolling, you start to prepare for next week. And the first step is updating your Value Ratings.

Updating NFL Value Ratings

To update your value ratings, simply compare the final score of the game to your projected point spread and adjust the Value Rating for each team according to Table 5.1. As an example, consider a game between the New England Patriots and the Denver Broncos, with the Patriots playing at home. Assume that before the game, the Patriots had a Value Rating of 105 and the Broncos had a Value Rating of 96.

Your projected point spread, using the Value Ratings, would have forecast the Patriots to win by 12 points (the Patriots' Value Rating of 105 plus the 3-point home field advantage minus the Broncos' Value Rating of 96). Let's say the Patriots actually won the game by 34 points (41 points - 7 points). Thus the difference between the predicted margin of victory and the actual margin of victory was 24 points (34 points - 12 points).

Using Table 5.1, the Value Adjustment Factor for each team would be 4, because the difference between the actual margin of victory and the predicted margin of victory was between 20 and 24 points. So 4 would be added to the Patriots' Value Rating and 4 would be subtracted from the Broncos' Value Rating. Before their game with the Broncos, the Patriots had a Value Rating of 105, so after the game, the Value Rating for the Patriots would be raised to 109 (105 + 4 = 109). For the Broncos, their Value Rating would fall from 96 (their Value Rating before the game with the Patriots) to 92 after the game (96 - 4 = 92).

TABLE 5.1

Difference Between Predicted and Actual Margin of Victory	Value Adjustment Factor — Add for Winning Team/Subtract for Losing Team
0 to 4 points	0
5 to 9 points	1
10 to 14 points	2
15 to 19 points	3
More than 20 points	4

Table 5.1 reports that if the margin of victory is within 4 points of your projection, then no change would be made to either team's Value Rating. If the margin of victory is within between 5 and 9 points of your forecast, then the adjustment to each team's Value Rating would be 1. If it's 10 to 14 points away, adjust by 2 for each team. A difference of 15 points to 19 points would require an adjustment of 3 to each team's Value Rating. And if there's more than 20 points' difference, the adjustment would be 4 for each team. Moreover, the rating for the team in the top position on the Value Rating scale should be no higher than 113 and the Value Rating for the worst team should be no lower than 87, meaning that 113 is the ceiling and 87 is the floor for Value Rating scale.

Recall that Value Ratings are to be used as a "top-down" method to forecast point spreads. They provide a relative measure of the strength of each team, and you should update them weekly to gain a deeper understanding of how teams are doing as the season progresses: which teams are getting better and which teams are getting worse.

Above all, when adjusting your Value Ratings, understand that the mechanical adjustment method I have outlined is meant as a guide — not as gospel. Many random and unpredictable factors can influence the actual margin of victory for a game: weather, injuries, unusual plays. Since it is ultimately your own experience, knowledge and judgment that will determine your sports betting edge, you should evaluate all factors when determining the appropriate adjustment to each team's Value Rating.

Use the Box Score to Prepare a Score Sheet Analysis for Each Game Played

To make informed adjustments to your *Get In and Win* Value Ratings, you should prepare a Score Sheet analysis for each game played the previous week, as we did for Super Bowl XLVI in Chapter Four. This fundamental review of each team's actual game results compared to its projected performance provides valuable insight into how teams are really playing, as well as their areas of strength and weakness. From this analysis, you can identify the good, the bad, the lucky, the unlucky, the overrated and the teams on the rise as the season rolls along. It is also useful for forecasting future performance in each of the key statistical categories for future Score Sheet inputs.

Consider the NFL game played between the Saints and the Browns during Week 5 of the 2010–11 season. The major Las Vegas and Internet sports books had the Saints as a 12-point favorite, but the underdog Browns stunned the favored Saints and won the game 30-17. A Score Sheet analysis of game statistics reveals that Drew Brees, the Saints quarterback, uncharacteristically threw four interceptions during the game, two of which were returned for touchdowns by the Browns. While a "pick six" is the kind of exciting play that fans love to see and usually has a significant impact on the outcome of a game, it is unusual and occurs infrequently, especially when it happens twice to an All-Pro quarterback.

According to Table 5.2, the adjustment to the Saints' and Browns' Value Ratings would be 4 (the actual adjustment would depend on your own calculated point spread for the game), but adding 4 to the Browns' Value Rating and lowering the Saints' Value Rating by a corresponding amount is probably too extreme based on two plays that had a disproportionate impact on the game's result. Adjusting each team's Value Rating by 1 or 2 would be more appropriate.

It's Time for You to *Get In and Win*

There you have it. You now have all the information you need to create wealth while having fun in a way you never thought possible. Did you ever imagine that you would be able to make big money by following your favorite NFL teams and predicting the game scores? Well, you now know that you can. And you have the secret right here in your hands.

The secret is having the right information, interpreting that information correctly and being businesslike in your approach. In doing so, you will use the triumphs and victories of the NFL's best coaches, players and teams to help you achieve personal success, sports-guru status and wealth. That's why I wrote the *Get In and Win* Pro Football Playbook, so you can get in on the fun too and make money at the same time.

Winning money by wagering on sports is not difficult, but it does require a commitment. Winning takes information, judgment, discipline and time. Why time? Why, you might ask, can't you just jump right in, hoping to start raking in the big bucks this afternoon? Actually, you can. The trouble is, you will also lose many of your bets; it's a fact you have to accept. Nobody's perfect, and losing is part of winning. But with the *Get In and Win* System, *you will win more often than you lose*. So it is over time, not overnight, that you will really see the compounded benefits of your wins.

But to experience success you have to swear to yourself not to be an average person, at least as it relates to your sports betting activities. Sports wagering is a zero-sum game — meaning that for every dollar committed, someone will win the money and someone else will lose it. During the course of a season, the average sports bettor will lose more than he wins because of incomplete information, bad strategy and poor money management — but you don't have to be average.

In all other fields of life, it is taken for granted that some people do things better than others. Aaron Rodgers is arguably the best quarterback in the NFL. Bill Belichick is recognized as a great football coach. Warren Buffett is widely regarded as one of the world's best investors. And Vladimir Ashkenazy is renowned worldwide as a master pianist. Why would anyone think that sports wagering is any different? If you do it well, there is money to be made wagering on sports. Don't let the naysayers convince you otherwise.

Betting on sports is exciting and fast paced, requiring mastery of many situational strategies. To be successful, preparation and precision are essential. That's why it's imperative to have a well-thought-out game plan so you can execute flawlessly and score when the pressure is on. It is the precise execution of a proper process that produces winning results. *Get In and Win* has all the right plays, so you can wager with confidence when the game is on the line. When applied consistently over the long term, the *Get In and Win* approach provides the strategic advantage required to earn real profits in the sports betting market.

After applying the lessons learned in this *Get In and Win* Playbook to analyze team performance, predict NFL scores and place winning wagers, you will never view what is happening on the gridiron the same way again.

Go ahead and **Get In and Win** so you can profit from your passion for sports!

www.ingramcontent.com/pod-product-compliance
Lightning Source LLC
Chambersburg PA
CBHW061357090426
42743CB00002B/42